Meet Me in Laurel Hill

Why they met, who they met and was it murder?

by Carolyn Bless Larsen

AuthorHouse™
1663 Liberty Drive
Bloomington, IN 47403
www.authorhouse.com
Phone: 1-800-839-8640

First published by AuthorHouse   11/17/2011

ISBN: 978-1-4520-2645-9 (sc)
ISBN: 978-1-4520-2647-3 (e)

Library of Congress Control Number: 2011960696

Printed in the United States of America

Any people depicted in stock imagery provided by Thinkstock are models, and such images are being used for illustrative purposes only. Certain stock imagery © Thinkstock.

This book is printed on acid-free paper.

authorHOUSE®

Dedicated

To my children, grandchildren and siblings
for their help and support through the
writing of this book, as well as through
all of my life.

To my friend, Brenda Hamby,
who gave me the idea for this book and
who gave me moral support, comfort and lots of
"tea and crumpets" during my writing.

Preface

Photo: Jessica Larsen

Laurel Hill Cemetery, a lovely shaded spot atop a hill, provides cool breezes and a lovely overview of a large part of Weston. This quiet "City of the Dead" was originally named City Cemetery about 1838. Later, due to the many Laurel trees there, its name was changed.

It is here that most of the original Weston citizens were laid to rest when their life's work was finished. In its early years it was also a place for young swains to bring their best girls on summer evenings, to do a bit of wooing.

It is this cemetery that Confederate soldiers "invaded" to bury some of their dead. Union soldiers set up tents in the northern part of the cemetery and it was here that they also hunted a man they considered to be a traitor.

Here, in this hallowed ground you will find many a young child's grave whose life was cut short by disease or accident. Though they did not have time to contribute much materially to the town, for the time they lived they brought joy and light into the lives of those around them.

Those who rest here: businessmen, doctors, builders, Civil War veterans, lawmen, musicians, teachers, wives and children peopled and built the town of Weston. They gave it a personality and its place in the historical limelight.

These graves hold people just like us who lived, loved, laughed and cried. They carved a niche in the town for themselves and their families.

These were the "movers and shakers" of their time although most would have been surprised at being labeled such.

There are also those who helped, encouraged and gave support to the, perhaps, more notable ones.

As you read this book you will discover most of these folks were everyday, run-of-the-mill individuals, not saints; others had somewhat of a questionable character. While not condoning their misdeeds, one can still respect their drive, their ambitions and their accomplishments.

The main push for this book was a fear that the information would be lost to future generations. As these generations come and go, perhaps this book will serve as a reminder and an appreciation of those who preceded them in Weston's history.

Table of Contents

Where They Met

A Kansas City 150th Anniversary Grant allowed the Laurel Hill Cemetery Association to replace an old chicken wire fence with iron fencing and gates, while a gift from Mike and Ruth Marr of Weston made this hand-welded sign possible. The cemetery is unendowed and run by a board of volunteers.

A small part of Laurel Hill, perhaps a half acre or so, became a cemetery around 1838 and by 1853 was becoming crowded enough that T.F. Warner, at one time a partner to Ben Holladay, donated another three or four acres to the cemetery.

Originally the peaceful, scenic area was simply referred to as "city cemetery". Later on, due to the many laurel trees that grew there, it became known as Laurel Hill Cemetery.

However no laurel trees remain, in the cemetery or anywhere in town. No one seems to know what happened to them.

North Meets South

Photo: Weston Historical Museum

Jayhawkers of the Kansas 7th Volunteer Cavalry patrolled in front of Ilkenhan's Jewelry and Clocks on Main Street.

During the Civil War, Union Troops from Fort Leavenworth came by ferry to take control of Weston. Due to the town's proximity to the military post, the Union was not about to lose it to any Confederate troops.

Weston was a town known for its many southern sympathizers. Altogether there were between 1,800 and 2,000 volunteers furnished for the Confederate Army from Platte County, many from Weston.

The tearing apart of families which was so prevalent in the south due to one family member being "for the north" and another professing allegiance to "the south", was felt almost as deeply here in Platte County as in the southern part of America. Looting and threats occurred when someone felt a neighbor or former friend was showing too much preference to one army or the other. There were also shootings, burnings, hangings and beatings.

According to one legend a young lady with the last name of Glover, living with her parents on a farm just outside of Weston, saw Union soldiers take horses from her father's barn, including her own favorite mare. Incensed, the young woman walked the several miles to where the horses were corralled in an area of Laurel Hill. Before she was seen, she had mounted her mare and rode out close to the encampment of men singing "Dixie" with great enthusiasm.

It is told that the soldiers not only cheered her, but did not pursue her to recover the mare.

Another lady of Weston, when approached by a Union soldier for her horse said, "here, take him and good riddance. He has never been any good, no one can control him. I will be glad to be rid of the beast."

When she moved to shove the reins into the bewildered military man's hands he backed away, saying he "did not need a contrary horse. Keep it."

The lady turned her back to the soldier and with a small smile twitching at her lips, led the beloved horse back to its barn. She, too, lies in Laurel Hill.

Though it is true that many of the citizens came from the southern part of the country and it was also true that most favored the south, still many of them signed a resolution that stated "though we love the south, we love the union more." Thus it was something of a love/hate relationship that existed between the Union soldiers and the citizens of Weston.

Why They Met

The note was slipped from the small dark hand of the young slave into the large, white hand of the well-dressed man coming from his office. His hands had long, tapering fingers that held a great deal of strength. They were the hands of a surgeon. Dr. William T. Shortridge of Weston was a man of gentle but determined nature. The note in his hand said simply, "Dearest One, Please meet me in Laurel Hill tonight. (Signed) C.A."

Shortridge knew this note would appear to be an assignation with a lover. After all, he was a married man and Laurel Hill with its many trees and flowering bushes was often a trysting place for young lovers. In fact, if the truth was known, he had done a bit of "sparking'" there with his present wife while they were courting. Thus the note was made to appear as such.

However this was 1862, smack dab in the middle of the Civil War. Dr. Shortridge was determined to keep the Hippocratic Oath he had taken when he became a doctor and thus was also determined to administer medical aid to any and all who needed it or called upon him.

This note meant that tonight he would quietly slip through Laurel Hill, keeping far to the east side to avoid the Union soldiers bivouacked on the western slopes of the hill, meet a member of the Confederate Army (C.A.) and ride the horse he brought to an unknown destination. There he would try to help the poor devils who had been shot during a skirmish or perhaps administer to one who had become ill of typhoid, food poisoning or the like

The doctor did not look at this as "giving aid to the enemy" as he also gave aid to the Union soldiers who needed him. He refused to choose sides. He simply saw all of them as human beings and as such they deserved whatever he could do to help them in their discomfort, pain or dying moments.

William T. Shortridge was born in Georgetown, Scott Co., Kentucky on May 18, 1823. He took his medical studies in Kentucky and married Thomasella Bartlett of Lexington, Ky. Following her death in 1856, the young doctor moved westward, ending up in Weston, Missouri where he started a practice. He was well liked by the citizens and there was one in particular who enjoyed his company and the feeling was mutual.

Julianna McAdow was the daughter of another doctor of the area, Dr. Samuel McAdow. Julianna was totally enthralled by William A beautiful woman-child, and nineteen years his junior, Julia (as most called her) was sixteen years old when they married in 1858.

She was his adored wife and was treated as such by him. He took pride in the fact that she was not only the belle of all the parties but that she could ride a

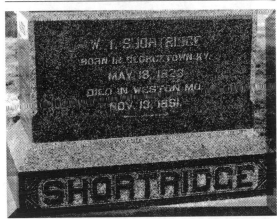

Doctor William T. Shortridge risked his life many times over during the Civil War because he took care of the wounded on both sides of the conflict.

horse as well as any man and was also a crack shot. In her younger years she had been something of a tomboy growing up in a family of seven children, but now, as a wife, she was always a lady.

When the Civil War came to Weston, Julia stood by William's side as he took care of the wounded. She helped to dress their wounds, fed them and allowed the use of her home as a makeshift hospital.

Growing weary in their attempts to set a spy to catch him, the Union officers one day threatened to burn their house. They demanded that Julia tell them where the doctor was. She refused, saying only that she knew him to be tending patients.

Julia and William had earlier lost two infant sons to childhood illnesses. Now she was nursing her third and last child, a very ill infant son. Losing patience with the officers who were keeping her from her son's bedside she told them, "Go ahead and burn the house if you feel you must, but you'll have to burn me and the baby too. I shall not move that ill child." They left defeated. The house and its precious inhabitants remained unharmed.

Eventually they caught the doctor on a night as he slipped away to take care of another Confederate soldier. He was arrested on the spot, his actions called "treasonous" and he was transported to Ft. Leavenworth. There he remained their "guest" for a time. During those months he later said he "was well cared and provided for, even playing chess with the commandant" at times. He also helped take care of the health of other inmates and soldiers alike.

After several months, William was given a release and sent back to Weston. The good doctor was needed here. The townspeople needed him. His family needed him. The Union soldiers needed him. They began to turn a blind eye to the times they noticed him missing from their midst. He was too good of a doctor, too

Photo: Weston Historical Museum

Mrs. Julianna McAdow Shortridge was called the tomboy of the family. "Whatever those McAdow boys did, I did too. Nothing was too tough for me to try." As an adult however, Mrs. Shortridge was every inch a lady and a most gracious hostess.

dedicated a man to put in jail or to execute. Upholding his Hippocratic oath, he made it safely through the rest of the Civil War and through the unrest and poorest years following that conflict.

Shortly after his return from Ft. Leavenworth the Shortridges lost the battle for the life of their last child. William and Julia became even more devoted to each other and to the people of Weston.

Dr. Shortridge died November 13, 1891 and was buried in the part of Laurel Hill that was a cemetery. Julia met the good doctor again when she was buried next to him and their children upon her death February 15, 1935.

Who They Met

Slowly, in a group, they walked up the street towards Laurel Hill. There had been a promise made and now they were all to meet there. One of their own, Henry Scholssner, had been laid to rest and the lovely metal monument he had designed for himself was complete. They would see to its placement on his grave site.

Henry T. Schlossner was born in St. Petersburg, Russia during January 1805. Nothing was known of his life in Russia. Except, that is, that he had been a Czarist soldier at one time.

Henry left Russia and came to America. It was not known how or why he had eventually found his way to Weston, but he was here and here, he said, was where he would stay.

What was known about Henry was that he was well liked, a good friend to "walk the path with". He was known to say that his past was exactly that – past –and his new life in a new country was all that held any interest for him. He wanted to be a good, productive American.

Schlossner designed and built the first 'Gas Works' building for the town,

which was quite pretentious and ornate. Set six feet back from the sidewalk, it was trimmed with iron grillwork on the stairs and porch.

When construction was completed, the town's citizenry celebrated with a torchlight parade and a large banquet.

In front of the building, at the outer edge of the sidewalk, Henry erected an ornamental light post of iron. It stood for many years on what was originally Water Street (now known as Market Street), even after the building itself was razed.

Henry lived at the back of his building. He was always impeccably dressed and groomed even when wearing old work clothes. He never married but always enjoyed visiting with the ladies and he was unfailingly courteous. He was a cheerful man and stood ready to be helpful to any who needed his assistance in any way.

A faithful member of the local Masonic Lodge, Henry designed his own monument, requesting of his Masonic brothers that they have it built out of metal and placed on his grave. He died December 13, 1869 and this was their last

In the northwest corner of Laurel Hill Cemetery sits the monument of Henry T. Schlossner, a Russian immigrant, who died in 1869. The Masonic Order of Weston erected this metal marker, which Schlossner designed himself.

"meeting" with Henry as they carried out their promise to him

The workmanship is so detailed that people mistake it for a marble tombstone, but one need only tap on it to hear the sound of an empty metal chamber.

Henry Schlossner's monument has been photographed and written about in several national magazines.

Friends Meet

Photo: Bless Collection

Cemeteries in the early 1800's were not the cause of fear or foreboding sometimes attached to them in modern times. The tough settlers of this community accepted death to be as much a part of the natural flow of living as the births which started us all on this journey.

Though they paid for a cemetery lot with "perpetual care" and the cemetery did have it's own sextons, families too felt it was their obligation to attend to their loved ones' graves. Especially after the War Between the States, cemeteries became gathering places for families on beautiful sunny Sundays.

Following services at various churches families, usually several generations strong, would drive to Laurel Hill to cut the grass and tend to the plantings. They would also see to the care of gravesites of those who had no descendants still living in Weston. After decorating the grave with seasonal flowers they would enjoy picnic lunches while seated on blankets and camp chairs brought for the occasion. As the trees in the area were not as mature as they are now, you could view downtown Weston, or look across at the old Weston Academy on the next hill.

Children were allowed to play, running among the headstones playing tag or hide-and-seek, their laughter ringing throughout the area. The gentlemen in the group, replete from their repast, might lie back and enjoy a nap, as the ladies would sit and reminisce about the dearly departed and the lives they had led.

Throughout the afternoon, all the families would visit with one another, discuss the weather and activities of the community before heading home as the sun settled over the hill.

Was It Murder?

Photo: Weston Historical Museum

Frank Kelly, along with a partner, bought the St. George Hotel and opened up "Kelly's Bar", which he ran until his death.

People would often meet in Laurel Hill as they went to place flowers on loved ones' graves. They stopped at the grave sites of friends and this was especially true as they passed the site of Frank and Josephine Hollied Kelly's last resting place. It was inevitable at such times that two or more would begin to speculate about Josie's demise.

Frank M. Kelly was born September 13, 1862. A big bluff Irishman, good looking and something of a dandy, Frank made many a lady's heart skip a beat or two when he chose to turn on his charm and Irish wit.

In his twenties Frank operated a grocery in Weston with W.H. Garrett for about seven years. As he turned the ripe old age of 37 Frank, along with George Baker, bought the St. George Hotel and Frank took over the Palace Sample Rooms from John Ryan.

The saloon's name was changed to Kelly's Bar. Later his brother, M.A. Kelly, had a pool-room directly behind the saloon. That end of the hotel later became known as Kelly's Landing.

Some time during his years with the saloon, Frank took up with a character called "Bennie". Of uncertain parentage, somewhat down on his luck and ready to find himself a "sucker," Bennie latched on to Frank. Bennie was a small stray dog, quick of mind and possessing a friendly demeanor.

Frank and Bennie became great friends and Kelly spared no expense in outfitting his friend with a wardrobe of clothes made especially for him. He even ordered a derby hat for Bennie from a leading Kansas City hat manufacturer. Due to the "oddity" of the order, the company had to send an expert to Weston to take Bennie's measurements. Other than the hats, Bennie's outfits were usually made by Helen Kenney, a young girl who lived with her parents in Weston.

Bennie's picture was used on postcards and in advertising for the saloon and the dog became widely known. Just when the dog died or where he was buried is unknown. It is known that Kelly was inconsolable upon Bennie's death and never had another pet.

On April 20, 1905, at the age of 43, Frank married Miss Mary Josephine Hollied, who was commonly known as "Josie." She was ten years Frank's junior.

In June of 1906, Frank shot and killed Josie thinking she was a burglar coming in a window.

"It happened thusly," according to

Frank. Josie had gotten out of bed about two in the morning to close a window in the bedroom because of the rain. Frank woke, saw a shadow at the window, called out twice to Josie but when she did not answer he thought it was a burglar, drew a gun from under his pillow and shot with deadly aim. Josie died instantly.

When he was called, the town marshal heard Frank's story, and saw no reason for an inquest. To his way of thinking no further investigation was needed. Nothing more was to be done.

Was Frank inconsolable over Josie's death? It was not recorded. However, he never remarried.

He was laid to rest beside Josie at his death from diphtheria on February 26, 1917.

Friends often wondered, when Frank met Josie again, was she angry or pleased to see him upon his arrival in Laurel Hill? And was Bennie nearby?

Photo: Weston Historical Museum

Bennie, in all his glory, is ready for a St. Patrick's Day party at Kelly's Bar.

The Laurel Trees

The laurel trees which had graced the cemetery from the beginning gradually died off. Pine trees, red buds and other varieties of trees were planted by the sextons who watched over the cemetery. Some trees and bushes came up voluntarily. In the late 1800's Fred Hollied, a local nurseryman, advertised that he had plantings "suitable" for the cemetery.

Streets had been laid out in the original plans for Laurel Hill, with such names as "Cypress Avenue" and Rose Bud Avenue" but they were never constructed and the proposed lengthening of Main Street to enter at the back end of the Cemetery never came to fruition. The cost to bring the road up the steep hill and through the cemetery was deemed too high for the benefit. Oddly enough, the roadway that has been in use for years has never had a name.

Over the years many families with loved ones buried in Laurel Hill would bring plantings from their homes which took root in the form of iris, peonies, lilies and other perennials. These were cared for by the families and if no one remained to take on the task the sextons would see to their pruning and care.

In the early 1970's large clumps of those plantings, some of which had survived for 75 to 100 years, were sprayed by an over-zealous caretaker and they all perished. Due to modern techniques of grounds-keeping it was deemed best to not replant them.

Was He Only Teasing?

Julius Rumpel and Dr. W. J. Simpson and their wives often met strolling through Laurel Hill in late spring and early summer. The view from the cemetery was a truly lovely and peaceful one. There was also the fact that they had friends and family buried there. The Rumpels and Simpsons enjoyed many outings together both in town and going to other destinations such as St. Joseph, Kansas City or Leavenworth.

Both men were born in Weston; Julius on September 7, 1862 and William on August 25, 1854.

As a boy Julius loved to hang around the business houses of his day — the packing plant, the mill, the furniture factory and the hemp markets. It was from his early observations there that he learned much of the acumen that made him one of Weston's most influential and successful businessmen. Though he left school early he never stopped learning, being a voracious reader and a shrewd observer of people.

In 1901 Julius Rumpel established the first telephone system in Weston which quickly grew until it spread over a wide network of country lines. In 1908, in partnership with B.J. Bless, he built the first tobacco warehouse where farmers could offer their crops for the inspection of buyers — the forerunner of the auction markets. He and Bless built the elevator and mill on the old Leavenworth Road. It later became the Farmers Cooperative Elevator. Also with Bless he began to build or renovate houses and buildings to encourage new businesses.

Rumpel believed in "giving back" to his community and did so in many ways. He worked for and with the Weston Fire Department, inventing several items to improve the fire fighting abilities of the

Photo: Bless Collection

Believing his friend and physician, W.J. Simpson, was having an affair with his wife, Julius Rumpel returned to his home on Washington Street and shot Dr. Simpson on the front porch.

volunteers. He was also chairman of the welcoming committee for the men coming home from WWI. Later Rumpel became the genial owner/manager of a saloon on Thomas Street. His peers considered him a well-met, intelligent fellow, always ready to help others and simply a comfortable chap to be around. Sometime before his purchase of the saloon on Thomas Street Julius was married to Addie Hinkley.

In 1880, W.J. Simpson married Cora Belle Mack and they had three children, two girls and a boy whom he adored. Besides being a physician, Simpson was active in the community and in 1890 became the president of the Weston School Board. He was known to the citizens of Weston as a upright, pleasant and honorable man. He had a warm teasing manner towards his patients, his friends and their wives as well as their children.

On the night of June 3, 1904, Dr.

Photo: Weston Historical Museum

Cora Belle Mack and Dr. W.J. Simpson married in 1880. Her daughter, Allie, granddaughter Marjorie and great-granddaughter Carole are pictured with her.

Simpson stopped in Rumpel's saloon for a bit of draft beer. He also enjoyed visiting with the patrons and the owner. That evening just before the doctor left the saloon he picked up a Royal Brewery mug full of beer. The souvenir mug had a verse on it and Simpson reportedly read the verse aloud to Rumpel:

> *Here's to the man who loves his wife,*
> *And loves his wife alone.*
> *For many a man loves another*
> *   man's wife,*
> *When he should be loving his own.*

Simpson finished reading the toast, took a few more drinks from the mug and left the premises with a wink and a nod toward the owner. From there he walked to the Rumpel home to check on Mrs. Rumpel who had been under his care of late due to an unspecified complaint.

After the doctor left, Julius considered the toast and came to an unproven and fatal conclusion. Leaving the saloon in the hands of an able clerk, Julius quietly followed Simpson. As Rumpel reached the front porch and started towards the door, he found Simpson coming out. Julius drew a gun and shot Simpson in the head, killing him. He claimed that his wife, Addie, and Dr. Simpson were having an affair and that he shot the doctor to defend

the honor of his wife and his home. There was no going back. The gentle friend, the good doctor was dead. Several days later Simpson was buried in Laurel Hill.

August of that year saw Julius Rumpel being tried for first degree murder by the State of Missouri in front of a jury of his peers. The trial had gone on all day in the sweltering heat; the courtroom was packed. At 10:00 p.m. on the evening of August 10, 1904, the case went to the jurors for a decision. A half hour later the verdict was read: "We, the jury, find the defendant not guilty." Cheers and congratulations were heard being shouted in the hallways.

Even though Rumpel had promised Addie he would not leave her if she testified to the affair, Julius sought and was granted a divorce in 1905. Two years later he married Blanche Sebus.

Despite his many successes in life and the fact that his fellow citizens held him in great esteem, Julius lived with great remorse over the killing of his friend Dr. Simpson.

In March of 1936, thirty-two years after shooting his friend, Julius died and even on his death bed he was heard to ask, "Was I wrong?"

Did he and William Simpson meet again in Laurel Hill as friends?

Photo: Bless Collection

The Simpsons built this house on Spring Street in 1895. A 2010 fire destroyed it.

Caretakers

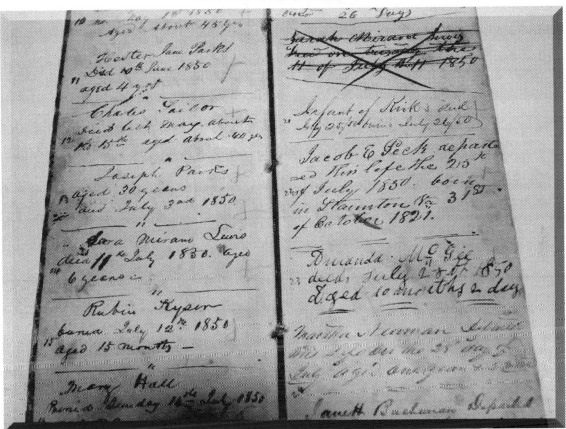

Photo: Jessica Larsen

Handsome, yet often-times illegible, hand-writing and poor spelling made sexton's books, such as the one above, difficult to read.

A caretaking association for Laurel Hill was established in 1915; D.M. Railey was the first president of the organization in 1920. In 1926 two and a half more acres were added to the cemetery by purchase.

While the cemetery was still under the auspices of the city, there were sextons who cared for the land, the graves and records. One of these was C.S. Thorning.

Another one, among several colorful sextons, was Peter Seeger. It made no difference the time of day or night or the season; hot or cold weather, Peter always wore a thick bright red wool shirt for digging graves.

Photo: Bless Collection

Peter Seeger was a Sextant for Laurel Hill Cemetery. He, too, rests in there.

Wild West Shoot-out?

Donald H. Weigman had served the City of Weston several times as marshal or as night watchman and it was in the latter capacity that he met his death shortly after midnight on Sunday, March 10, 1940.

Weigman was born in Weston October 23, 1902 and was married to Opal Allen in December of 1931. Don was educated in Weston and spent all but about nine years of his life in the town of his birth. For those nine years he was a special detective for the Frisco, the Union Pacific and the Kansas City Terminal Companies in Kansas City.

On that fateful spring night, Don had taken his wife home shortly before midnight telling her that he would be home in about an hour for supper. He dropped into the Henry Brothers Restaurant, where eight patrons were having a midnight lunch at the rear of the room separated from the front by a lattice.

After telling two of the patrons it was time for them to go home, Weigman sat down at the end of the counter in the front room.

One Henry brother poured a cup of coffee, as he had many times before, for the night watchman. At that time Henry saw one Mr. O.D. Gray come from the rear of the restaurant.

Gray leaned over the counter and said something to Weigman. Henry could not hear what was said between the two as they spoke quietly to one another, but he saw Weigman grab or shake Gray.

Then came a sound of popping. Thinking it was grease popping, Henry turned to see what was wrong on the stove as plaster began to fall on his face from the ceiling. Then came the sound of a larger gun.

Henry dove behind the refrigerator as he tried to disappear from sight. Gray fell

Photo: Bless Collection

At one time a detective for the railroad, Donald H. Weigman later became Weston's night watchman.

dead where he stood, three bullets having entered his body. There was a large wound to the head, one to the lung and a third to the abdomen. Weigman staggered to the front door and out into the middle of Main Street where he dropped. He had also been shot three times. Wounds were found in his neck, heart and leg, all on the left side. The wounds had been made with a .32 caliber pistol. Weigman had been carrying his usual sidearm, a .38 caliber.

Both the Platte County Sheriff and coroner were called. Upon viewing of the bodies and questioning of the witnesses, it was concluded that no inquest was necessary. The facts seemed to stand by themselves.

Weigman was buried in Laurel Hill. In later years none of his family, wife nor son, was buried next to him.

The Henry Brothers Restaurant sat where Weston Cafe now stands. Prior to that, Noble Motors Co. ran their Ford, Lincoln and Fordson dealership out of the storefront. The entire building was owned by M.R. Waggoner, who purchased it in 1914. The apartment in the upper right was where he and his wife Emma lived with their family.

Old-timers in Weston speculated that the shoot-out was over a love affair that Weigman was carrying on with Gray's estranged wife. Others believed that Weigman "had something" on Gray and had earlier been taunting him with it.

Though no one really knew the reason for the gunfire, in later years Peter Gray, O.D.'s son, said his mother did have an affair with Weigman. However, one must take into consideration the fact that Peter loved to shock people and he also loved to gossip, true or not. Either way, it left two widows and two sons to mourn the losses of their spouse and father. Peter was five years old at the time and Donald Weigman's son was six.

So, was it an affair, blackmail or something else the two men shot it out over? We'll never know!

Photo: Jessica Larsen

There are many broken stones scattered throughout Laurel Hill Cemetery. Volunteers and board members hold clean-up days where they try to repair, clean and locate stones. The unendowed cemetery accepts donations of all sizes to help with its care.

Laurel Hill has many unmarked graves within its wrought iron gates. Some of those are unmarked due to the finances of the family who lost a loved one. Some, too, are due to deterioration of the marker from outside influences such as weather, benign neglect and vandalism. Other graves are unmarked because the deceased ones were unknown to anyone around at the time of their deaths.

An example would be a notation in the sexton's records of 1866-1885: "Child, Unknown, about 8 months old, a White child found dead, one and one quarter mile below Weston on K.C.C.B. Railroad."

Another entry said simply "A Spanish woman, died Nov. 20th, 1851." Another was "Stranger buried, off of boat, May 29, 1852." And yet one more example "Infant died on a Boat. 20th day of November 1852." There were more: "A Mormon, 30th of March 1855." And shortly after that entry we find this one: "A Mormon child died April 11, 1855." There was no one to ask, no one to say to whom these dead ones belonged or from whence they came.

When cholera hit Weston in 1851-1852 it was no respecter of age, race, creed or gender. Entire families were wiped out in days. Parents were left bereft; children were left orphans; spouses struggled on without their other half. When the dread disease hit, families would hide the ill one in barns, sheds, even in the woods and take care of them there due to the fear of spreading the disease. Some of the unmarked graves are from those whose families brought them in "at dead of night" and quietly buried them in unmarked graves. Perhaps they intended to put up a marker later but possibly they died too. Or perhaps they were just too busy going on with broken hearts, struggling with diminished finances to afford any sort of marker.

Photo: Jessica Larsen

Aaron Harris' stone was toppled from its base during a vandalism spree. It has since been repaired.

Who Were They?

A re-enactment of the Battle of Bee Creek took place on the actual site of the skirmish in the mid-1990's. Casualties from both sides of the Civil War were rumored to be buried secretly in Laurel Hill.

With the horses hooves muffled by rags tied to their feet, the men crept slowly and as quietly as possible under dark of night toward the main gate of Laurel Hill. In the dim light from the stars and moon above, one could see that there were bundles tied over the saddles of some of the horses. The men wished they could have used a wagon but knew that would make too much noise for their purpose.

"They" were the Confederate soldiers who had earlier that day fought in a skirmish, perhaps it was the Battle of Bee Creek between Weston and Platte City, or some other engagement, when they came upon a troop of Union soldiers. Whatever the event, these men were doing their best to honor their fallen comrades. The "bundles" were the bodies of five men who had died in battle.

Once inside the main gate, the men slid down near the fence line in the front.

Seeing no monuments or markers of any sort, they felt assured that they would be laying their comrades in ground that had not been used by others. Digging swiftly and as quietly as it was possible, the five were quickly taken from the backs of the horses, already having been wrapped in their blankets, and laid to rest in unmarked graves. The living kicked weeds and leaves, twigs and grass over the area to camouflage where they had dug. Perhaps they stopped to say a quick prayer or two and then it was time to leave as quickly and quietly as they had come. At least one or two of them may have promised himself that he would come back when the war was over to put up a marker so others would know that here rested an honorable soldier, that he meant something to someone, somewhere.

It is documented that a young boy saw this and ran into town crying that someone was either digging up graves or burying someone. As far as anyone knows, little attention was spared for the young boy who most likely was admonished to go home. It was late and he should not have been out. Later an old lady who lived near the cemetery told her family not to bury her near the front fence, just inside the main gate, as she did not care to be buried near "those soldiers".

There are a few citizens who believe that some of the Union dead had also been buried in Laurel Hill but far to the back on the northwest slope where once they had an encampment. Though no graves have been recorded as such, it is possible that there were some buried there without markers. This could be due to a determination to remove the bodies later for a proper burial in Fort Leavenworth. It is unknown if this was done.

Perhaps years later the Union and Confederate dead met in Laurel Hill without anger or any vestige of animosity, much as some of the old veterans had done. They were, after all, simply men following their consciences, doing what they perceived as their duty.

The Markers

In the early days of stone statuary for grave markers, many were in the shape of tablets. They were often fashioned of native stone, white soft marble or field stone. Before that, families used crosses handmade from whatever material came to hand. Some used large boards with the essential information burned into them. After 1900 granite was most often the stone of choice.

As the years went by, the earlier simple stones and other markers gave way to larger and more elaborate monuments. Sometimes with larger stones an entire family of mother, father, daughters and sons were memorialized on the same marker. Then too, sometimes a family was fortunate enough to have a large monument with just the family surname emboldened upon it. Each member of the family would then have a smaller stone with their name and date of birth and death close to the main monument.

People began to insist on more elaborate stones and as time passed, a book of cemetery symbolism was "written" or at least passed into tradition. A stone with a hand that had fingers pointing upward meant that the deceased had, hopefully, gone to heaven. A draped urn was a symbol of mourning A stone in the shape of a tree trunk that had been cut, meant that the individual's life had been cut short in death. A hand holding a sheaf of wheat symbolized a fulfilled life; ivy symbolized fidelity and eternal life.

Lambs and small angels or cherubs were often used on graves of very young children. Adult angels were messengers and attendants of God, symbolizing they were sent to accompany the soul home. Not infrequently one sees an adult angel bent over seemingly in tears, mourning the loss of the loved one. In some cemeteries when a fatal disease took many young children from the midst of their families, there was a section called the "babies cemetery". Along with these sad and painful burials, there were long lamenting obituaries in the local newspaper bemoaning the loss of these "little ones".

The "Little Ones"

Only the actual obituary can really do this justice. Therefore, from the pages of *The Weston Chronicle* we read about the death of little Ethel on January 23, 1899:

Gone Home.

Little Ethel, the eight year old daughter of Mr. and Mrs. L. C. Stabler, died of pneumonia, at their home two miles east of town, just at the break of dawn, on Monday last.

Once more the shadow of death, once more the sky so lately bright and beautiful is oe'r cast by threatening clouds—a dear little form is missed by all—a sweet little face has vanished and the Sunday school misses it, the teachers and little playmates miss it, but oh!

How it is missed from the family circle can never be told. How broken and desolate is the home! How the little sister will long for the sweet face and merry voice of the little one who has been transplanted in God's flower garden on the beautiful shore. How that little brother will miss her merry childish romps; how that devoted and loving father will miss his darling at every turn!

But oh! There is one who will miss little Ethel more than all these, that mother, who lies on her sick bed, will recall every little act, every glance of the laughing eyes, every expression of joy or grief that crossed the little face of her baby, for little Ethel was "only a baby" though intelligent beyond her years.

She was a regular attendant of the Christian Sunday school and was beloved by pastor, teacher and classmates. . . she was conscious of her approaching death, and selected her own pall bearers, Messrs. J.W. Cox, Ed Hughes, W.C. Polk and H.C. Cunningham. . . And now a "little one" is snatched from our midst..."Safe in The Arms of Jesus" her feet had only trod the flowery path. She is spared the great suffering and heartaches that will come in one's path as they toil on life's rough road.

"Did we know the baby fingers
Pressed against the window pane;
Would be cold and stiff tomorrow,
Never trouble us again;
Would the bright eyes of
    our darling,
Catch the frown upon our brow
Would the prints of rosy fingers
Vex us then, as they do now?
Ah! Those little ice cold fingers
How they point our memories back
To the hasty word and action,
Strewn along our backward track!
How those little hands remind us,
As in snowy grace they lie,
Not to scatter thorns, but roses,
For our reaping, by and by."

Annie, the daughter of Joseph B. and Susan O. Davis Evans, died June 13th, 1857 at the young age of three. Her infant brother, Joseph, died in 1839.

The remains of little Ethel were laid to rest on Laurel Hill, there to sleep until the dawning of the New Day."

The daughter of Eliza and Fielding Burnes died June 26, 1868 at the age of ten months and two days. Inscribed on her stone:

"Thou art gone from me, sweet one. Father protect her, and her kindred spirits, when they arrive, no other help have they.
– F.B."

In one of the sexton's record books, under the heading of CHOLERA the names of many "little ones" are listed:

Died between Weston and Parkville, 3 o'clock morning of the 27th of May, 1851, on board of the Steamer "Alton" J.V.P. Bonfils, Jr., only son of Dr. & Mrs. J.V.P. Bonfils of Cholera. Aged five years and 3 months. Born in Saint Louis, Mo. of American parentage.

Mary Halpen died 31st May 1851 aged 9 years.

Phoebe Jane Hartly died 12th June 1851. Age 11 years.

Elizabeth Long died 14th June 1851. Aged 13 years.

Luciana Norton died 14th June 1851. Aged 2 years.

C. Norton died 17th June 1851. Age 4 years.

Mary Long, died 14 June 1851. Aged 12 years.

Lewis Deerer died June 17th 1851. Aged 3 years.

James E. McKinney died 19th June 1851. Aged 10 years.

L.L. Bird died 26th June 1851. Aged 14 years.

Mary Norton died 27th June 1851. Age 13 years.

Mary Park's infant child aged 6 months. Died 30th June 1851.

Louisa Eiser died 30th June 1851. Age 8 months.

Charles Waller, died 30th June 1851.

Photo: colorado-cemeteries.com

A stone similar to this once stood at the grave of Eva Marie Bless, who was but one month old at her passing. Years of weather took its toll, making it necessary for the family to replace it.

Aged 11 months.

George Buckler died 30th June 1851. Aged 1 year & 6 months.

Infant child of Wier, died 4th July 1851.

Cummings child, age 8 months. Died 14th July 1851.

Saul English aged 2 years. Died 18th July 1851.

Nevada L. Carrier, parents unknown, was 6 years and 4 months of age when she died on April 12, 1884, at two o'clock that afternoon. She had been born in Tennessee. Her cause of death was pneumonia and croup according to her attending physician Dr. J.W. Martin.

Donald D. Moore, son of Mr. and Mrs. B.F. Moore was eight years old at the time of his death on Sunday evening July 22, 1904. He had been down with appendicitis and had undergone surgery for it by Drs. Redman, Smedley and Willis of Weston. The operation seemed to be successful but the little fellow succumbed anyway. It was thought possibly from infection that had set in.

Due to virulent children's diseases, accidents, poor health of the mother or poor health of the child when born, the list of "little ones" buried in Laurel Hill is quite lengthy.

A Piece of Their Hearts

Courtesy: Weston Historical Museum

Many of Weston's early citizens eventually moved on to other towns.

They moved because of the unrest during the Border Wars and the Civil War. Some moved out of fear of the marauding elements in the area. Others were ordered to move.

There were others who simply moved on due to wanting new challenges, new outlooks, needing more room to breathe as civilization expanded.

Whatever the reason was for moving on, wherever they traveled from here – north or south, east or west, many were brought back to Weston to a final resting place in Laurel Hill.

It might have been because there were already loved ones buried here. Perhaps it had something to do with the sentiment voiced by one individual to an old friend about his desire to be buried in Laurel Hill: "Weston has a very special, tiny bit of my heart and always will."

A Land Planner

General George Washington Gist, born in 1795, arrived in Weston in 1846 from South Carolina. He was a surveyor, interested in real estate, and new challenges.

One of Gist's descendants was South Carolina's "Secession Governor" William H. Gist, who will long be remembered as the man who led South Carolina into secession which in turn encouraged other southern states to follow suit. They then formed the Confederate States of America and the rest is history.

George Gist, however, was not particularly interested in secession, states' rights or slavery. He was interested in lands that could be surveyed and turned into busy towns and cities. George enjoyed the challenge of this, never letting heat or cold or other pesky things, such as Indians, turn him from his goal. He founded The Leavenworth Company in Weston and then crossed the Missouri River to survey the land for a city to be called Leavenworth. He laid out the streets and with others in the Company he began to sell lots there. In time George moved there with his family.

Gist had instructed that upon his death he wished to be taken back to Weston and buried in Laurel Hill. At the time of his death in November 1854, Leavenworth had one hotel, one sawmill, one tailor, one shoemaker, one barber, two blacksmiths,

Photo: Jessica Larsen

General George W. Gist was a land surveyor who came from South Carolina prior to the Civil War. He is buried in the northeast corner of the cemetery.

one newspaper, three lawyers and two doctors.

It could be said that George Washington Gist wanted to meet up with old friends and neighbors in Laurel Hill when he made his request to return here.

A Destitute Man

Another gentleman who moved away from Weston but requested his body be interred in Laurel Hill was Jacob Mettier.

Born in Germany in 1822, Jacob dabbled in Weston politics and was a licensed attorney. But at heart, he was a confectioner. Much more than a baker, a confectioner made such things as almond macaroons, bon bons, pound cakes, petit fours, cookies and the like.

Jacob married a young lady by the name of Anna, but after three years of marriage, and believing Anna had been unfaithful, Jacob filed for divorce. They reconciled and he dropped the petition. The couple went on to have seven children, but only two survived to adulthood.

The building in which the couple made their fortune in Weston still bears their name, and almost anyone in town can point out the Mettier building today. A three-story brick building on the west side of Main Street, the first floor was used as the bakery and salesroom; the second floor for a ballroom; and the third as the banquet room.

Large receptions for weddings and other special events were held in the hall. Dances and balls for the young elite of the town were enjoyed. Mettier furnished the refreshments, which were called collations and they were nothing short of a small banquet. Dishes such as cole slaw, celery, pickles, relishes, oyster stew, potatoes, dumplings and several types of meat were offered. Desserts consisted of homemade ice cream, cakes, cookies and pies of every variety.

Jacob welcomed many members of the military from Fort Leavenworth; quite a few romances began in the ballroom between young ladies of Weston and the dashingly uniformed officers.

Some time after accumulating their

Drawing: Weston Historical Museum

The Mettier (pronounced meteor) building remains one of only four 3-story structures in downtown Weston.

small fortune, Mettier and his wife left the business in charge of a friend and went to Europe to visit family. Upon their return they found the "friend" had run through the money. Jacob was bankrupt.

He vowed to start anew but with the tenor of the times and Civil War looming, business was not as brisk as it was before. Mettier decided to remove to Leavenworth and start again.

In 1852, a heavy storm did considerable damage to the building he had constructed on Shawnee Street. Because of that and the hardships suffered during the Civil

In 1851 Mettier added a "Genuine Soda Fountain" to his shop. Although he was a successful businessman, an embezzling employee ruined the Weston business and Mettier and his family relocated to Leavenworth.

War, Mettier never regained his fortunes.

He died in Leavenworth on July 29, 1899, a broken man. His wife honored his request and had his body brought back for burial at Laurel Hill in the town he always claimed as home.

Anna followed him to this last resting place in 1911.

Was It Jealousy?

The body of Alexander M. White was brought to Weston to be buried in Laurel Hill, by the side of his father, the late James O. White. The date was June 22, 1917 and White had not died from natural causes.

Though born and raised in Weston, at the time of his death Alexander was living in St. Louis. He was a musician and a member of the famous Arthur Pryor band. He was considered to be, next to Pryor himself, the best trombone player in the world.

White met his fate at the hands of a jealous landlord who believed that Alexander was having an affair with his wife. The man, in a jealous and murderous rage shot Alexander in the back as he was shaving in his own bathroom. Alexander was forty-five at the time of his death and had never been married. At a coroner's hearing following his death, Alexander was exonerated of any wrong doing. We know nothing about what happened to the landlord or what became of the wife.

The Masonic burial ceremony was conducted at the grave site and included

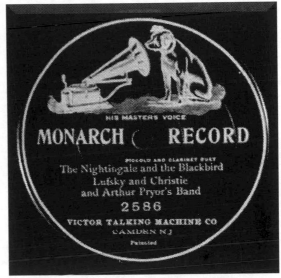

Courtesy: Arthur Pryor Collection

Alexander White played with Arthur Pryor's Band until his death in 1917, appearing on many of his recordings.

John U. Dale, George Spratt, J.H. Brill, Canby Hawkins, John Thorn, Oliver Cox and Charles Hillix all of Weston. Mrs. Mahlon Gabbert of Weston was listed as a survivor.

Though she was not born here, this fair lady was well-known to Weston residents and they considered her "one of us." In her turn, Grace was always loyal to Weston.

Grace Marie Breen was born and grew up in Parkville in a house her father had built on Main Street. Grace was the youngest child and only daughter of Charles Patrick and Mary Noll Breen, who had started married life in Weston. Even though they moved a few years later, the Breen family remained connected to the town in many ways.

Grace lived a life that reached into three centuries, having been born in 1898 and living until 2004. She was born in a time of horse-drawn buggies, elegant manners and strict morals. She lived to see "the mob" do its worst to Kansas City and its environs. She knew of the Kansas City Union Station Massacre; the Pendergast regime; and the Truman years. She saw such wonders as the first gasoline-powered vehicle, the Model-T Ford and later the stretch limo. She was around to hear about the flight of Wilbur Wright and later flew on jet airliners.

The shoot out that ended the careers of Bonnie and Clyde in 1933 was at the Red Crown Tavern on old U. S. Highway 71. At the time, the tavern was owned by Grace's brother, Emmett. She was living when a man in a jet plane broke the sound barrier and when a man first walked on the moon.

Grace could remember hearing her father talk about the sinking of the steamboat *Arabia* and then followed news accounts of its excavation many years later. She was here when the *RMS Titanic* sank and lived through World War I and II, the Korean War, the Cold War, the Vietnam War and the Gulf War.

Photo: Nancy Jack, The Southern Platte Press

Grace Breen enjoyed teaching for over 50 years. This enthusiastic and much-involved woman was born in 1898 and died at the age of 106 in 2004.

Grace was born when William McKinley was president and she lived to discuss the merits of George W. Bush as a president.

Charles Patrick Breen, a stone mason, built Holy Trinity Catholic Church in Weston, using stone from the quarries on Park College grounds. When he would come to work, many days his young daughter, Grace, came along with him to watch and to play with her young friends here. She would pack a lunch for the two of them and though running off to visit with friends, she always came back to enjoy lunch with her "Papa". Grace also took catechism classes at the parish house and made her First Communion at Holy Trinity.

Grace attended and graduated from the Parkville Public School. She later was

Photos: Weston Historical Museum

Parish members attended the 1912 dedication of Holy Trinity Catholic Church in Weston at the beginning of its construction. Grace Breen's father "Pat", at right, was the stonemason who built the church.

enrolled in Loretto Academy in Kansas City, a private school for girls conducted by the Sisters of Loretto, graduating in 1917. Grace went on to receive her Bachelor of Arts degree from Park College and earned a Masters degree in Speech from the State University of Iowa in 1938.

It was as a teacher that Grace excelled and really made her mark in life. In 1921 she went to work for the Kansas State School for the Blind and for the Kansas City Conservatory Drama Department. In 1940, she was offered the position of teacher of speech at East High School in Kansas City, later transferring to Southwest High in 1946 where she taught until her retirement in 1970.

Some time during the first World War, Grace worked briefly at the Farmers Exchange Bank in Parkville — her family owned the bank — filling in for her brothers Ed and Emmett who had enlisted in the Army. During World War II, Grace saw many of her young students leave for service in their country's military. She wrote letters to many of them, kept in touch with their families and prayed for all of them. She again worried and prayed about her young students who served during the Korean and Vietnam Wars.

At the age of 102, Grace took up the game of bowling, and as usual doing nothing in half measures, established herself as a high scorer.

Miss Breen grew up in a Victorian atmosphere, learned to be a "lady" and remained so all of her life. Her basic message to students remained relevant throughout the years: "Enunciate clearly, speak distinctly and know what you want to say." She served as an example of her own belief that one could change with the times and still remain a lady or a gentleman.

Upon her death in 2004 Grace Marie Breen, at her request, was brought to Weston to be buried in Laurel Hill to meet again with family and friends.

A Teacher and A Friend

In this June 1916 photograph, Miss Honora Allen, left, and Miss Mary Allen, right, stand amongst the bank of daisies at their home, "Sunny Slope."

Once one met Honora C. Allen, one felt as though they had made a friend for life. Honora was born in Weston January 5, 1869 in a little home on West Walnut Street to parents from Ireland. The home continued to be her place of refuge for 66 years.

Honora received her education in Weston schools, then in summer terms at Chillicothe, Missouri University, Kirksville and finally, Warrensburg, where she was awarded a degree in education in 1928. She spent 47 years in the classroom, having taught in the rural schools of Beverly, Cox and Hazelwood. She also taught at Brinktown School near St. Louis and the St. Vincent Orphanage in Leavenworth, Kansas. Weston, however, claimed the major part of these years of service.

Miss Allen, who never married, was a lovely lady who made friends with all of her students, keeping up with their comings and goings in life long after they had graduated from W.H.S. She was also active in her community, church and school. She helped her sister, Mary, spread the lovely Madonna lily bulbs to many gardeners in Weston, thereby creating thousands of lily blooms each spring to the delight of residents and visitors alike.

As well as a public school teacher, counselor, friend and guide, Miss Allen is remembered as the promoter of some of the finest home-talent shows that have ever been seen in Weston. Thrifty in her own nature, she was just as thrifty for all who participated and few people before or since have been able to bring as much net proceeds to the school or church or community as did Miss Allen with her beautifully staged events.

Honora died in 1941 and was buried next to her sister and brother in Laurel Hill. She had entrusted to a friend the money to see that she had an appropriate headstone; but several years after her death it was discovered that the "friend" had absconded with the funds.

The word went out to former students, fellow teachers and friends who wished to visit the site of her burial. Funds began to pour in for a simple but lasting marker for a woman who had befriended many and had been such a 'shining star' in their lives.

This one stalk of perfumed and nearly-perfect blossoms of the "Madonna Lily" was from the Allen garden. Due to the ladies' efforts, the lilies could be found in almost every church yard and home garden in Weston.

A Doctor's Tale

Dr. Thomas Beaumont was born in Yorkshire, England on December 12th, 1811. He came to America at an early age and received his medical education at the Pennsylvania Medical College. Following his graduation he chose to "go west" and ended up in Weston, where he soon became a busy physician.

Beaumont had married a Miss Nace while in Pennsylvania. She died shortly after the marriage, leaving him a widower.

The good doctor married three other times; twice to Weston women (Mary Emerson and Lucy Sandford) who also died early in their unions. Beaumont's final marriage was to Amanda Hunt Queen of Platte City. Upon his death on September 22, 1871, he was buried in Laurel Hill

Thomas was the father of six children, one daughter and five sons. During his time in Weston he owned several homes in and around town. One of these homes was a large, two-story brick house on Spring Street, just west of the Weston Historical Museum, now owned by Mrs. Jean Hartley.

Dr. Beaumont was an active member of the Weston Christian Church. He was also the president of the Board of Trustees for the Orphan School in Camden Point, being very devoted to the children there.

On the day of his death, Dr. Beaumont was discovered dead in his horse-drawn carriage on the road between Weston and Platte City. There seems to be some mystery as to the cause of his death. No witnesses were found and authorities refused to answer questions. There was some speculation as to whether it was of natural causes or if he might have been robbed and shot. Or, did he simply succumb to a heart attack?

He is buried in Laurel Hill near several of his wives.

Photo: Weston Historical Museum

A well-respected medical doctor of Weston, Dr. Beaumont met his death in a manner never revealed by his family or the authorities. Was he murdered?

An Accidental Merchant

William H. H. Ohlhausen was a steamboat engineer who later became a miller.

Born at New Market in Platte County on September 12, 1841, William was a bit of an adventurer and enjoyed plying the Missouri River as an engineer on steamboats.

After spending twelve years on the River and while docked at the harbor in Weston one day, a local banker asked Ohlhausen to take charge of the engine at the Weston Mill. Due to mechanical and financial problems, the owner was unable to continue, and William soon became a part owner of the business. Such a life seemed to agree with him and he eventually became the sole owner.

At the age of twenty, William married Miss Harriet Johnston who was born in London, England on April 25, 1844. The couple had four sons, Charles Alexander in 1862, John Wesley in 1864, Edward Lee 1867 and William in 1884.

For 35 years William owned and operated the flour mill, which was located on Washington Street. He became close friends with many of the farmers of the area, who would bring their families into town to shop for necessities such as flour and meal.

Flours of various grades and composition were ground at the mill. Perhaps the most famous of those were the three called "Sun," "Moon" and "Star." The Sun

Photo: Weston Historical Museum

The front facade of the Weston Mill, the grain storage building and mill house are all that remain of what William H.H. Ohlhausen, in white, managed on Washington Street. The rest of the building was destroyed in a 1987 fire.

flour was used for cakes and pastries; the Moon was used for breads; and Star flour was for general purposes. Housewives loved having the different grades of flour for their needs. Folks bought their flour in sacks of 25 and 50-pound weights.

The Mill thrived under Ohlhausen's management and one could often see long lines of wagons waiting to have their various grains ground into flour and meal.

An active man in his community and church, William joined the Presbyterian Church in Weston in 1877 and became an elder in the church in 1880. He proved to be a good neighbor and was always ready to help his community and his fellowman in support of good enterprises.

Harriet, his wife of nearly 56 years, died in January 1917; and even though William continued to be involved with the Mill and enjoyed watching his grandchildren thrive, he missed his life-long companion. Five years to the month after

Photo: Weston Historical Museum

This grindstone was installed by William Ohlhausen at the same time he built a separate building for the storage of grain.

her death, William again met Harriet in Laurel Hill, where they now lay side by side.

Militia Surgeon

Dr. Benjamin Bonifant, as did several other physicians in Weston, believed strongly in his Hippocratic Oath. He was thought to be a southern sympathizer by some, a Union supporter by others, but he nursed or aided Confederate and Federal alike.

Benjamin Bonifant was born in Montgomery County, Maryland February 15, 1821 to John and Mary Tucker Bonifant a young farm couple. During his youth, he worked the farm with his father, but medicine was his ambition. He attended Medical College in Philadelphia. In 1850 Benjamin migrated west, settling in Weston three years later. During the Civil War he served as the surgeon for the 4th Missouri State Militia.

He married Miss Matilda J. Leachman in 1855 and they had two daughters. One, Mary, died at birth and the other, Ada, married Rudolph O. Shenkner, who was a successful businessman in the mercantile business in Weston.

Dr. Bonifant was known to the medical profession of almost the entire mid-west and was called the "Father of Surgery" in this part of the state. He had a gruff exterior but was very kind and gentle with his patients.

A partner, Dr. Oscar F. Bowers, died in 1859 leaving all of his property to Dr. Bonifant so as to continue as a physician in Weston.

Benjamin died at the age of sixty-eight in August 1889. He was buried in Laurel Hill next to the wife to whom he had been deeply devoted during their lives together.

Many funeral services held by the Weston Masonic Lodge were quite elaborate. A horse-drawn hearse, the one above owned by S. Renz, was escorted by uniformed members as it made its way to Laurel Hill Cemetery.

The Other Holladays

Phena Calvert was born in 1834, the younger daughter of Smith Calvert and Phena Johnson Calvert, and married David Holladay on January 14, 1851.

She was the second daughter that Calvert had "lost" to the Holladay family. Notley Ann, her sister, had eloped a year earlier with David's brother Benjamin, who became the well-known "King of the Overland Stage" later in life.

Phena and David's first home still stands today, on the northwest corner of Spring and Summer Street, now owned by Bill and Connie Jurgens. The two-story brick home had slave quarters and other buildings on the property.

Just as her husband was quiet and reserved compared to his flamboyant brother, Phena was the opposite of her sister. She was a serene and capable hostess for the busy, industrious David, who built and operated the Holladay Distillery, now known as McCormick Distillery.

The second Mrs. Holladay in Weston, Phena not only needed to keep up with her husband's many entertainments for out-of-town businessmen, she also had to manage the household and the half dozen slaves they owned at the time. Phena was not known to "put on airs" as did her sister, but remained the same as she had been in her early years, calm and matter-of-fact.

David and Phena seemed truly devoted to one another and in time five children were added to their household. Though she had capable help in the home, Phena spent a great amount of her time caring for and guiding her children through their formative years.

Unlike that of her husband and famous brother-in-law, Phena's death on April 5, 1898, caused no big stir outside of Weston, but her family and friends greatly

Photos: Weston Historical Museum

David Holladay and Phena Calvert married in January 1851, one year after her sister eloped with his brother. Phena was a year younger than her sister, but considered herself much more mature.

missed her in their daily lives.

Some said David was heartbroken without her and others said he just refused to go on after her death. However it was, David met Phena again in Laurel Hill upon his death a year later in 1899.

A True Pioneer

Photo: Weston Historical Museum

From Illinois to Missouri to Utah, Hannah Gilbert and her family led the lives of pioneers.

Hannah Pasto Gilbert of Joliet, Illinois, married a man from Hastings, Canada and came with him to Weston in 1839. At that time Abel Gilbert was twenty-seven years old. Hannah was a hand full of years younger than her husband.

During their early years in Weston 1839-1857, Hannah was busy with the births and the raising of seven children, six boys and one daughter. Abel became a successful businessman in Weston and slowly became involved in the Salt Lake City trade with the Mormons. For several years Abel made the trips across the plains with others, then hired others to make those same trips for him.

The Mormons, who seldom trusted "outsiders", seemed comfortable with Abel and felt they could trust him. Hannah, with her love of life, her hospitality and interest in their lives and the tenets of their belief, was another reason they trusted Abel.

In 1857 Hannah and Abel took their children and trekked across the plains and sands to Salt Lake City where Abel set up shop, trading solely with the Mormons. The trip by wagon to Salt Lake took 28 days. Some of those days were quite harrowing, including several scary encounters with the Indians along the trail. Hannah was frightened for her children as well as for herself and her husband. She made little protest however against this move. She felt it was best to keep all of her family together, no matter where Abel wanted to wander.

Once in Salt Lake they were treated as "outsiders" but eventually they won the trust of the people. This was again due in great part to Hannah who treated the Mormons as she would have liked to be treated and expressed an interest in their lives and beliefs.

Though a "gentile" she was invited to watch as the great Mormon Temple and Tabernacle was built. It was an experience Hannah never forgot, and she loved telling friends and family about it.

Hannah, Abel and their children again made the long, tiresome and somewhat dangerous trek, this time from Salt Lake to Weston in the late 1860's. Abel again set up shop as a mercantile in Weston. Though he was successful both times in Weston as well as Salt Lake, Abel began to see his fortunes going down hill. Upon his death in December 1871, Abel left little property to his family, but he had given his children finished educations and promising starts in their lives. He was buried in Laurel Hill.

Hannah lived to be nearly 100 years old, dying June 25, 1910. She met Abel again when she was laid to rest beside him in Laurel Hill.

A Wanderer Comes Home

Born in Germany in November 1822, Frederick Olendorf started his "wandering" when he emigrated to America at the age of 23.

At first he served as a government agent and then a translator during the U.S - Mexican War. After the war, Fred relocated in Illinois, where he lived for 15 years. With his wife Sophia, a Prussian immigrant, he moved to Weston in 1865.

Mr. Olendorf was one of the later settlers of Platte County and lived just north of town. A prosperous farmer at the time, he and Sophia had eight children, two of whom died at young ages in 1867.

The couple was highly esteemed, being well liked by neighbors and other Westonians. Upon the death of Sophia in 1882, Fred began to experience reverses in his fortune. He seemed lost without his helpmate and began to roam from place to place. In 1899, in his late seventies and in increasingly poor health, Fred eventually made his home with his daughter, Sophia, and her husband, Henry Helman of near Weston.

At the time of Olendorf's death, his children were also scattered around the country: son Ernest resided in Council Bluffs, Iowa.; second son, Charles, lived in Jackson, Michigan and Albert, his third son, lived in Los Angeles, California. Fred's other daughters, Mrs. Lou Chalfan lived in Missouri Valley, Iowa and Mrs. Amelia Raymond resided in Battle Creek, Michigan.

Olendorf joined his wife in Laurel Hill on Friday, March 2, 1900.

Photo: Weston Historical Museum

Frederick Olendorf's grave, like many others in Laurel Hill, has lost its marker due to age and erosion so it is unknown exactly where he was buried. Also like others, his family has moved out of the area or died out and there is no one to care for it. The Laurel Hill Cemetery Association was formed to help in the upkeep and repair of the cemetery.

A Builder of Dreams

Frank Haas and his partner, John Hollied, built and renovated houses in the Weston and Bean Lake areas. The one above was constructed at the corner of Rock and Walnut Streets for his cousin, William Haas, in the late 1800's. The structure was torn down in the 1980's.

Frank Haas was born near Weston May 3, 1874, a son of Woolf and Frances Green Haas. A man who worked with his hands, a builder of dreams for others, Frank built many fine homes in Weston. He built them to last and many of them have. Those that did not survive the years were ones that either burned or were torn down to make way for something newer

Frank attended Weston schools and graduated from Weston High School. In December 1910 he and Miss Vita Kirkpatrick of the Bean Lake area were married. The young couple enjoyed fishing, swimming and other such pursuits with other couples in the area of Bean Lake. They became the parents of two daughters, Orene and Vivian.

For many years, Frank had a partner, Mr. John Hollied. The two of them not only built homes and other buildings, they also did remodeling, painting and were general all around handymen. The two gentlemen took pride in their work and it showed in the finished product. It still shows today in many of the homes in the area.

Friendly, cheerful and constantly working with his hands, Frank loved his work and he loved people. He retired shortly after the death of his wife in 1944. Vivian died a few years later. Elderly, and beginning to have health problems, he moved to the Leavenworth home of his surviving daughter, Mrs. Orene (Edward D.) Pepper.

Frank enjoyed coming back to visit in Weston with his friends and to "check out" the homes he had built in his younger days. On January 7, 1965 he died at the home of his daughter, leaving six grandchildren and eleven great-grandchildren. At his request, he was brought back to Laurel Hill to rest beside his wife.

Alone, But Not Lonely

Maude, the only daughter of Thomas G. and Clare Holladay Barton was born in Plattsburg, Missouri in 1881. As a young girl she moved with her parents to Weston and remained a resident the rest of her life.

During her younger years, she was frequently a visitor in the home of her grandparents, David and Phena Calvert Holladay. Maude's grandfather built the original stone building at the center of the McCormick Distillery campus.

Educated in Weston schools, Maude later attended the Sacred Heart Convent for young ladies in St. Joseph. She also attended several fine schools for young women on the east coast.

Her great-uncle, Benjamin Holladay of stagecoach fame, was quite fond of his niece and she was a frequent guest in his palatial homes. One favorite, Ophir Farm in New Jersey was her home for several months at a time and she reveled in being amongst the many cousins who came and went. Ophir Farm later became the summer White House for President Calvin Coolidge.

Courted by and married to Frank A. Poss of near Beverly, the couple made their home in Weston. Maude was a young matron of the town and loved entertaining their friends at dinners, musical evenings and other parties.

The couple had one child, Barton, who died without a wife or child. Frank had died several years before Barton and both her parents passed shortly thereafter, leaving Maude with no immediate family.

To help fill the void left by the deaths, Maude befriended many, especially the young people of town. She was always ready to hear about their exploits, their dreams and plans. She watched carefully their comings and goings, always inter-

Photo: Weston Historical Museum

Maude Barton Poss dressed up for what was called a "Tacky Party" with friends. With her husband and only child dead, Mrs. Poss threw herself into the community and became confidant to many in town.

ested in all that life brought to them.

In her later years, Maude experienced ill health and became something of a re-

cluse in her home on Market Street hill. Born into a family of wealth, she lived to see those fortunes lost over time, but the love of graciousness and fine things remained with her throughout her life. She often said "I'd rather be poor and know about and appreciate the arts and not be able to have them, than to be rich and never recognize the finer things in life."

Maude Barton Poss died on December 11, 1961 at the age of 80 years and was buried in Laurel Hill near her son.

Barton Poss was the great-grandson of David and Phena Calvert Holladay. He died in 1944 at the age of 32.

Last of Her Line

A descendant of Daniel Boone, Robert E. Lee and Colonel James Price, Forestyne Marie Loyles was the last of her line. Five generations of her family had lived in the ancestral home on Spring Street in Weston, and the house held many antiques, much history, and was filled with many journals and diaries written by the inhabitants. They chronicled the times and lives of those who had lived in the 3-story home, as well as the comings and going of Weston citizens.

Born May 24, 1907 Forestyne was the only child of Irene "Tootsie" Guthrie and Frank Loyles. A beautiful child with long golden ringlets, Forestyne possessed a vivid imagination. She loved to dress up and play make-believe even to the point of writing elaborate plays, which she presented to her mother.

Perhaps she got her sense of drama and acting from her father, Frank, though she saw little to nothing of him. Frank, being an aspiring actor, drifted towards California, returning on few occasions.

Forestyne was stricken with polio at an early age, causing her to wear a brace on her affected leg, yet she remained active, feisty and full of good humor all her life. She turned into a lovely, attractive young woman and had many beaus as well as many would-be suitors had "Mama" allowed it.

Irene Loyles was a domineering and demanding mother, refusing to turn loose of her only child. Though Forestyne would have loved to be married, travel and have a real life, she sacrificed herself to her mother's demands. Rather than defy her, Forestyne remained most of her life in Weston.

She was active as the President of the Weston High School alumni association in 1932 and a few years later she became

Photo: Weston Historical Museum

Forestyne Loyles was a mainstay of Weston businesses, working as a telephone operator, a receptionist, bookkeeper, secretary and a stint as Weston City Clerk.

a dramatic director for would-be actors and actresses in Weston, putting on many elaborate theatrical productions. She also was the City Clerk for a time, resigning from that position in 1955. She went to work in 1939 as a receptionist/secretary/bookkeeper for Missouri Public Service and continued with them until she retired over twenty-five years later. Forestyne was a charter member of the Platte County Historical Society and of the Weston Historical Museum, being named a trustee of the latter in 1969.

Two of the great events in her life were the rare finding of lilacs blooming in her yard in the chilly November of 1941 and attending the 1951 opening of Kansas City's Starlight Theatre. The theatre

The Prices-Loyles house was home to five generations of Daniel Boone's descendants, the last being Forestyne Loyles. The home recently went through a renovation and attempts have been made to recover many of the family's historical pieces.

had always beckoned to Forestyne but "Mama" successfully squelched the following of that dream. Thus it was a delight and a comfort to Forestyne to attend each and every performance possible at the Starlight until her death in 1991.

A courteous, helpful and personable employee, Forestyne also exhibited a wry sense of humor to those who knew her. For the last ten years of her life Forestyne was confined to a wheelchair but never lost her sense of the ridiculous or of fun.

She loved opening her home for mini-tours and on other special occasions, delighting in sharing her family's history with visitors and friends alike.

When Forestyne was buried in Laurel Hill among her family, she surely must have enjoyed meeting her illustrious ancestors. One can imagine her writing a special play and perhaps coaching them to join in her fun.

An Orphan Finds A Home

This house on Edward Street was the home of Nimrod Houser, an orphan to whom family became paramount. Currently the home of the Sanchez family, the house was originally two rooms on each side of a long hall. Other owners of the home have been Mr. and Mrs. William Helvey, Mr. Floyd Bramble and Mr. and Mrs. Larry Hamby.

Nimrod Houser was born somewhere in Ohio and at a very early age he became an orphan. Until he was about twelve years old, he made his home with grandparents and upon their death he lived with other relatives until he reached young manhood. He then chose to travel further west into Iowa for a few years before coming to Missouri and then Weston. He later met, wooed and married Miss Mary Blanton. Mary, born December 19, 1853, was the young daughter of Warren and Sophronia Blanton. Mary and Nimrod were married November 17, 1874.

Nimrod and Mary soon had four sons, Thomas, Warren, Allen and Neal, making a close knit and loving family. As he worked at his livery barn on Thomas Street, Nimrod's heart and thoughts were wrapped up in his family and home.

Having been deprived, at an early age, of the closeness of parents and siblings, Nimrod never took for granted either the love or the needs of his family.

An outgoing personality, he made friends quickly and was always ready to help any one of them who needed something from him.

"Nim" died Thursday, August 22, 1913, at his home on Edward Street and services were held there the following day by Rev. Marion Moore with interment in Laurel Hill.

Nimrod did not wish to leave Weston, nor his family and home. In Laurel Hill he would always remain near them.

Among The First

Born in Mount Sterling, Ky., on June 13, 1814, Tabitha Cumi Davis first met and later married her husband, John Breckenridge Wells in the same town. They were married in April of 1832. John was 14 years older than Tabitha.

A year after their marriage, the couple emigrated to Marion County, Mo. and early in 1837 they came to Platte County where Weston became their permanent home.

While her husband was busy with his steam ferry at Rialto, which served as the highway to and from Kansas and beyond from 1854 to 1865, Tabitha was busy at home with all the attendant chores a housewife faced in that era. She was also a very busy mother to their nine children. Their firstborn, a son named Leander, was reported to be the first white child born in Platte County.

At the age of fifteen or sixteen Tabitha made

Drawing: Weston Historical Museum

The first Methodist Church in Weston, shown in this drawing, was located on Short Street, behind what is now Mc-Calley's on Main Street. It was built in 1842, with the initial funds given by Tabitha Davis Wells. The congregation continued to meet there until a new and larger church on Main Street was finished in 1867.

a profession of faith in the Methodist church in Kentucky. She was one of the founders of Methodism in Weston, giving the initial one hundred dollars to build a frame building on Short Street. She was in attendance to hear the first sermon preached in this house of worship and she remained a member for more than 70 years.

It is also said that Mrs. Wells was given the privilege of naming the streets of Weston. Her life span covered the period from the beginning of settlement in these parts to shortly after the beginning of the 20th century, having outlived all the other pioneers whose names are associated with the history of the county.

A close and loving couple, Tabitha mourned her husband for the nearly ten years she was a widow. She died January 3, 1903 and following services conducted by the Rev. F. J. Maple, pastor of the Methodist church, her remains were interred next to those of her husband in Laurel Hill.

Accompanying his widowed mother from Kentucky, Joseph Anderson was only four years old when they arrived in Platte County in the year of 1849. His farmer father had died shortly after Joseph's birth on May 10, 1845.

Settling near New Market, Joseph was schooled at home for several years and then became an agriculturist, a career he followed until the outbreak of the Civil War. Joining the Union forces, he served in the Eighteenth Missouri infantry. He fought in a great many battles, among them those at Shiloh, Corinth, Kenesaw Mountain, Peach Tree Creek and Atlanta, Ga.

At the latter engagement, July 22, 1864, Joseph lost a limb and was sent to the hospital, where he remained until he was honorably mustered out of the service in 1865.

While on a furlough home on March 24, 1864, Joseph married Nancy Turner. Following his mustering out, he returned to his adopted state of Missouri and moved to Weston. He gave his attention to various occupations for some time, including the offices of constable, township clerk and justice of the peace.

Nancy died September 27, 1893, leaving Joseph to mourn her and to care for their eight children. He was nearly inconsolable at the loss of his wife, but knew he must continue on for the sake of his children.

He became the manager of the Exchange Hotel in Weston, meeting with good success.

Eight years after the death of his first wife, Joseph married again, to Mrs. Rebecca Murdock, a woman from St. Joseph. They had five years together before Joseph developed heart disease and died February 14, 1906, leaving his wife and four living children to mourn him.

He was buried from the Weston Baptist Church, where he had been a member for over 35 years, with services conducted by Rev. Lee Harrel. Burial was in Laurel Hill under the auspices of the Odd Fellows Lodge.

Joseph Anderson and his wife, Nancy Turner Anderson, were buried side by side in Laurel Hill. Joseph was severely injured in the Civil War.
Photo: Jessica Larsen

A Progressive Mayor

Martin Richard Waggoner arrived in Weston in February 1898, opening a jewelry store on the lower east side of Main Street. After a few years. M.R., as he was known, left the business to begin work as the manager of Kelly's Saloon where he introduced some innovative changes.

Following a short courtship, M.R. and Miss Emma Quinley of Weston were married on January 2, 1910. Their first son, George Richard, was born in December 1910. The couple lost him at the tender age of two. Their second child, Martin Richard, Jr., was born several years later and survived into adulthood.

Waggoner announced he was running for Mayor in the spring of 1921. He won the April election in 1921 and thus began twelve years of great change in the City of Weston. A gentle man of large stature, Mayor Waggoner was often seen in town in his black suit, gold watch and chain and sporting a wide-brimmed black hat.

Following a few months of orienting himself, M.R. enthusiastically promoted "Dollar Days" for Weston. Merchants and citizens alike were pleased with the results. Waggoner worked with the editor of the local newspaper to urge the citizens to clean up the streets and empty lots in and around the town.

In 1926 it became apparent to everyone that the town desperately needed paved streets. With a population of about 1,000 people, Mayor Waggoner realized the assessed valuation of the city would not bring in enough funds to pay for the contractors' required costs. So he began investigating prices for the machinery that would be necessary for such work.

With the backing of the council, he purchased electric drills, a rock crusher, a concrete mixer and asphalt tanks. By hiring

Photo: Weston Historical Museum

M.R. Waggoner used innovative ideas to get paved roads for Weston while he was the mayor. He also served as Platte County Clerk.

good laborers, paying good wages and demanding good service, M.R. was able to save the Weston taxpayers hundreds of dollars. When he found it necessary, he donned work clothes and turned his hand at mixing cement, crushing rocks or whatever chore that was needed.

During the next few years the Mayor and crew resurfaced every one of the old macadam streets with paving. He also inaugurated a system for keeping the streets clean and repaired.

Waggoner again personally helped when a bridge needed to be built on Thomas Street over Mill Creek. Constructed in 1926 the bridge stood for 80 years, finally being demolished in 2006 to make way for a broader structure.

Again showing his acumen as a businessman, he oversaw the laying of several blocks of water mains; a White Way containing 50 poles; and management of the municipal water works. In his years as Mayor, Waggoner also reduced the city's indebtedness by over $20,000.

Hoping to bring more monies into the city coffers, Mayor Waggoner instituted the first Tobacco Show in 1921. This was held in one of the tobacco warehouses and was for citizens as well as visitors to the town. There were mock auctions to raise funds, a "Queen of the Tobacco Market", home-cooked meals, local musicians and participation by Future Farmers of America and 4-H chapters. These shows continued into the late 1950's and brought in not only money to the city finances, but lots of fun and entertainment for the Weston citizenry, as well as to those from neighboring towns.

His business sense and the improvements he made to the city were not his only accomplishments. M.R. could also sew and embroider and did so quite expertly. According to his wife and to others, he could bake a batch of biscuits as good as any woman. However, his greatest talent was his artistry with pen and ink. He would often decorate his letters with some clever cartoon or drawing relevant to the subject upon which he was writing.

In 1914 Waggoner bought a building on the west side of Main Street. He and Emma, along with their surviving son, lived in the second-floor apartment.

In December 1937, M.R. passed away and was buried near his son, George. His wife, who had encouraged, aided and pushed M.R. to greatness as a mayor, lived on in their apartment, watching life go on in the town they both loved. She remained a widow until her death in December 1979 and was interred next to her beloved M.R.

The Entrepreneur

Theodore F. Warner was one of the pioneer businessmen and settlers of Weston. Born in Greenup County, Kentucky on April 18, 1818, Theodore was a grandson of Daniel Boone and settled in Platte County about 1841.

In July 1844 Warner opened a store in the Rialto Bend area. It thrived for two reasons: the Rialto Ferry — run by John B. Wells — brought military men and area settlers across the Missouri River to purchase needed supplies, and because of Warner's energy and work ethic.

Several years later Theodore became a partner with the boisterous and flamboyant Ben Holladay. The two started their first venture, The Overland Express, freighting cargo and passenger traffic to the golden coast of California. They also transported supplies to Colonel Alexander Doniphan during the war with Mexico and freighted supplies to Salt Lake, Utah.

In 1861 when the Civil War began and the Pony Express ground to a halt, Warner and Holladay bought out the owners of that venture — Russell, Majors and Waddell.

The men carefully selected the strongest and fastest animals for their stagecoaches and they chose the Concord coach, which was structurally one of the best in the country.

Their empire continued to grow exponetially, reportedly reaching over 5,000 miles of stage lines. Warner and Holladay were wined and dined in cities across the nation.

Despite accruing great wealth, Warner grew tired of the constant traveling and the social events they were required to attend. He sold his interest to his partner Ben, who went on to become known as "The Stagecoach King", and he returned home to Weston.

Photo: Weston Historical Museum

Shortly before his wife's death, Theodore Warner was elected to the first of two terms as Platte County Clerk. It was the latest in a life full of service to Weston and Platte County.

Much like his grandfather, Warner wanted a quiet lifestyle in which he did not have to deal with huge crowds of people; he wished to stay closer to his humble beginnings. He wanted also to be nearer his wife, Emily, and their children. The couple lost several children in their early infancy and Emily had fragile health, acerbated by the worry and fear she had for the survival of their other children.

Warner became a silent partner in a line of steamboats which traveled on the Missouri River. Friends, family and even strangers considered him to be honorable in all of his transactions. A courteous, and a rather quiet gentleman, many citizens remembered "Uncle Theo's" frequent deeds of kindness, charity or words of encouragement.

In 1868, Warner was elected as a Missouri State Legislator, representing Platte County for two terms. Following this, he engaged in the business of Weston, working as a cashier for the old Platte Savings Institution.

During this time, Emily's health continued to decline and they traveled a bit in search of medical help for her. Despite everything, "Em" grew weaker and frailer with the passage of time. To add to his own anxiety over his wife, some of his investments began to fail.

Urged by his friends, he ran for and was elected to the Office of County Clerk in 1878. A year later, in 1879, his beloved companion Emily succumbed to her many illnesses, leaving Warner bereft without her presence and support. He served his four-year term and then accepted a second four-year term.

Wearied by this time and still lost without Emily, Theodore moved to Kansas City where he lived with a daughter and her family until his death in 1891 at the age of 73. His body was brought back to his beloved Weston for burial next to his "Em" and other members of his family.

A Woman Scorned

Born to Balthazar and Minnie Scheuttner How in 1864, Mary Elizabeth first met Bartholomew John (B.J.) Bless about the time she was six years old. Later she said she knew she had met the young boy who would eventually become the man she would one day marry. For Elizabeth, B.J. was her one and only love, or as she would put it, "the love of my life".

A petite, somewhat shy young woman, Elizabeth loved gardening, children and her church. She did not reach a full five feet in height and though mostly retiring, she was determined in many ways and would exhibit once or twice in her life a towering anger.

Through school years and several years when B.J. was working and living in Jefferson City, Elizabeth remained steadfast in her love for him. When he returned to Weston and after a few years of courtship, the two were married on October 4, 1887.

A son, Bartholomew Joseph Bless, (B.J., Jr.), was born to them on October 9, 1888. Daughter Eva Marie, was born in January of 1890. The tiny miss died the following month. There were no other children and the son became known as "Bartie" to friends and family.

Perhaps B.J. was just trying to live up to what people thought about most editors—they were drunks. Perhaps he was haunted by the death of his baby daughter. Whatever the cause, B.J. began to drink heavily. He bought a parrot and gave it to his wife as a gift one day following a bad drunken spell. He taught the bird to call out, "Lizzie! Lizzie! I need you!" Elizabeth did not like to be called Lizzie but B.J. did so often, affectionately and teasingly. The bird mimicked his voice perfectly so when it would call "Lizzie," thinking it was in fact B.J. and that he truly needed her she

Photo: Bless Collection

B.J. and Elizabeth Bless stand beside their home on Thomas Street prior to their divorce. After they remarried, she nursed his mistress through her final illness.

would run to the porch where the bird was most often found. She grew to hate the bird and even in the daytime, the bird and its cage were often found covered so it would think night had arrived and not call out to Elizabeth.

One day, about the time that "Bartie" turned nine years old, Elizabeth discovered that B.J. had taken a young lady, living in town, as his mistress. Bewildered, humiliated and angered beyond reason, she refused to take the insult. Throwing B.J. out of the home, she filed for divorce despite the views of her church, the feelings of her family and the snide remarks of others. Elizabeth obtained the divorce and continued to live in Weston as a single mother.

Leaving his workers to continue to produce the newspaper, B.J. and his mistress disappeared from town. Months later, Elizabeth began to receive letters from B. J. asking her to take him back. She refused to answer the letters until one day she saw the return address was from Menninger's in the middle of Kansas. B.J. was taking 'the cure" for alcoholism. He asked her forgiveness, promised to give up his mistress and said he needed her. She replied with one word, "NO!"

Eventually B.J. returned to town, without the mistress, seemingly cured of his drinking and took over the editorship of his paper once again. He continued to beg "Lizzie" to take him back. Fearing that something would happen to him, still loving him, Elizabeth finally agreed. They were remarried within the Catholic Church and took a second honeymoon.

Unbeknownst to anyone, Elizabeth kept tabs on the whereabouts of the former mistress. When she discovered the woman was seriously ill, possibly dying, and had no one to care for her as her family had disowned her, Elizabeth's compassionate and caring heart was stirred. She told B.J. they had to go to Lawrence to bring the woman back. She further informed B.J. that since it was his fault that this lady was an outcast, a fallen woman, he would have to stand for any medications and doctor visits needed. B.J. did not fight Lizzie over this. They brought her back, installed her in a bedroom in their home and Lizzie tenderly cared for her.

Sadly, the lady died. Her family refused to help with the burial, firmly making it known that she could not be buried in their plot in Laurel Hill. They didn't even want her buried in the same cemetery. B.J. then stepped up and offered to have her buried in the Bless family plot in Laurel Hill. His wife replied that there would only be one woman lying next to him and that would be Mary Elizabeth How Bless. With that she informed B.J. that he would have to pay the expenses to have his former mistress taken back to Lawrence, Kansas, where Elizabeth had found her and bury her there. She and B.J. traveled with the coffin and had the woman buried in Lawrence.

Life went on for Elizabeth and her adored B.J. Their son married, took over the newspaper and had children of his own. As the great-grandchildren arrived Elizabeth was in her heyday. She had three of her most beloved possessions around her — B.J., the great-grandchildren and her Madonna lilies growing profusely in the garden on Thomas street.

B.J. became ill in April of 1943, dying June 19, 1943. Lost without "the love of her life" and certain that he was waiting for and needing her, Elizabeth followed on August 22, 1943.

They repose side by side in Laurel Hill.

A Business Tycoon

Brothers Charles and E.H. Perry were partners in many and various ventures. Together they owned businesses, homes, freight lines and the steamboat "The Excel", which travelled the Missouri River.

Charles Perry was the gentleman who brought the hemp plant from Kentucky to Platte County, after having it checked out in a lab to see if it would grow in the soil of the area. Thus began years of hemp growing and individuals growing rich on the proceeds of it.

Charles Perry was born in Montgomery County, Maryland, on December 6, 1818. He was educated in the schools of the county. The summer after he turned 14 he went to Washington, D.C., where he began his business career with the firm of Cleary & Addison, a wholesale grocery business. He remained with them until he decided to move westward at the age of 21.

In 1842, he purchased a home in Weston and married Martha Ann Young of Shelbyville, Kentucky. The couple lived in Weston until after their two oldest children, Charles and Alverda, were born.

Charles then purchased property a mile from Weston on the Platte County Pike. Originally called "Oakland", its name was later called "Quality Hill Farm" because of the fine soil for raising tobacco. Three more children were added to the family, Arcadia, Florence and William.

Martha Ann died in June 1867. Perry later married his second wife, America Jane Hamilton, of Wilson County, Tenn. To this union was born four children, two of who survived beyond childhood.

Charles' younger brother, E.H. Perry, came west to join his brother in business, shortly after Charles came to Weston. The two built a mill near the mouth of the port of Weston. They supplied the government with many contracts for flour and other grains. They also supplied Kansas and Northwest Missouri.

Shortly following this venture, E.H. Perry moved to St. Joseph to take charge of Charles' active businesses located there.

In 1865, at the close of the Civil War, the Perrys furnished and delivered to the government, by overland wagon transportation, a large quantity of corn for which they received eleven dollars a bushel, at the crossing of the South Platte River, Denver City, Fort Halleck and other parts of the West. They accomplished this in less than twelve month and in return C.A. and E.H. Perry drew $2,000,000 from the federal government.

Charles had been elected in 1855 to the Missouri Legislature from Platte County with a unanimous vote and served several terms. Charles and his brother has also invested in the steamboat industry and actually owned the ship called *The Excel*.

Later, in 1872, the brothers became contractors for the labor of the convicts in the Missouri Penitentiary and Charles resided in Jefferson City for approximately three years. He then moved to St. Joseph and became president of the first Street Railway Company. He went east and ordered the equipment, saw the rails laid and the first car started on Frederick Ave.

After an active and varied life, Charles died in St. Joseph on November 16, 1896, just short of his 78th birthday. Despite his long absence from Weston, Charles wished to be laid to rest in Laurel Hill and this was done according to his wishes.

Perhaps he felt most at home among the other earlier inhabitants of Weston, and especially the businessmen he had known and socialize with in his early years in Weston.

The Silent City

Photo: Jessica Larsen

I visited the cemetery today where the people of Weston bury their dead. The imposing monuments that mark the resting places of many who sleep here, speaks of affection and remembrance. The inscriptions on these tomb stones tell of the expectation of a happy reunion in that great somewhere; we remember our dear ones as we saw them last, shrouded and laid in their sepulchers. The heart will accept no change, when the shadows of evening gather around we think of them, and in the fading twilight, feel the touch of a vanished hand. How our spirits yearn to bring the lost ones back, but death yields not to tears nor broken hearts; inexorable death thou shalt give back our treasures at last.

It is spring time again, the song birds are here, the earth swarms with joyous living things, the grass is green on the hillsides and the air is scented with the perfume of odorous things, nature is resurrecting, but sleepers sleep on. Never again will we see them this side of the dark river called the river of death, they are gone, memory perpetually reminds their sweet associations, the fond embrace, the good night kiss.

I wonder if any one who sleeps here were broken hearted, and death came to them as a benediction. I wonder if any who scatter flowers on them in the spring time have any regrets, because of neglected duties. What of the future while the dead sleeps on forever, Oh! No! It cannot be. A thousand omens give hope of a bright immortality. The imperishable desires and aspirations of the human heart are meaningless if it be not so.

The Weston Chronicle
May 22, 1903
By B.J. Bless, Sr., Editor

Bibliography

Annals of Platte County Missouri, by W. M. Paxton. Published by
    Hudson-Kimberly Publishing Co. of Kansas City, MO. 1897.

Family History files of The Weston Historical Museum, est. 1960.

Photography files of The Weston Historical Museum, est. 1960.

The Weston Chronicle, 1886 – 1980. Microfilm of the Bless family.

Weston, Queen of the Platte Purchase, by Mrs. B.J. Bless, Jr. Published by
    The Weston Chronicle, September 1969.

Index